DEVOUR EVERYTHING / SARAH STEWART

Devour Everything

Sarah Stewart

Published in 2026 by Tapsalteerie
Tarland, Aberdeenshire
www.tapsalteerie.co.uk

978-1-9192208-0-2

Printed and bound by Clays, UK

Poems in this collection have appeared in *Ambit, Best Scottish Poems, Butcher's Dog, The Honest Ulsterman, The Interpreter's House, The Keats-Shelley Review, Magma, Mslexia, The New Shetlander, Nutmeg, The Oxford Magazine, The Passionfruit Review* and *The Scotsman*.

Supported by the National Lottery through Creative Scotland

CREATIVE SCOTLAND
ALBA | CHRUTHACHAIL

LOTTERY FUNDED

For NSS

i

Illusory – 11
Talking to My Mother About Clothes – 13
Cluedo – 14
Horoscope – 15
Inspector Morse Extra, 1989 – 16
Second-Hand Dress – 17
A Deliverance – 19
For the Mother in the Crowd at Shea Stadium – 20
Heliotherapy – 21
Portraits of Lizzie – 22
Knapping – 25
The Sonographer Sees the Complication – 26
Sylvia Plath as Heart Surgeon – 27
Beam – 28

ii

Caddy Lamb – 31
Revenant Visits Her Old Bedroom – 32
Sales Pitch of an Honest Estate Agent – 34
Anatomy of a Painting – 35
Opening Scenes of a Never-Made 80s Thriller – 36
Dinner on Ithaca – 38
Self-Portrait as Submariner – 39
Kidnap & Escape – 40
Blackbird – 42
Ghazal for a Small Town – 43
Animal Magnetism – 44

Domestic – 45
Japanese Wind Telephone – 46
Afternoon Tea in a Time of Horror and Chaos – 48
Blót – 49

iii

Life Model – 53
This Is a True Story – 54
Bellville, TX – 56
Swimming – 57
The Dead Go to the Theatre – 58
Icarus as a Girl – 60
Cassiopeia – 62
On Suburbia – 64
Son, it's 7pm in April – 65
Sweetheart – 66
The Charity Shops of Aberdeen – 67
The Calligrapher – 68
Man with Hidden Face – 69
Vesta Surveys Pompeii – 70
The Patron Saint of Lost Things – 71
Miniature – 72
The Pantone Colour of the Year is Green 2252c – 74
56.9° North – 75
The End – 76
Pienza – 77
Mijas Pueblo – 78

i

Illusory

> 'Our everyday life is only an illusion, behind which
> lies the reality of dreams.' – Werner Herzog, *Fitzcarraldo*

In the way that you turn a corner on to a street
you knew when young and catch your breath:
its dimensions calcified, unchanged

in the way that a stuck door creaks open
to reveal a garden full of honeysuckle,
sheened with snail slime, netted with cobwebs

in the way that orderly rooms, scrubbed clean,
lose their patina of interesting dirt –
watermarks, spilled ash, candlewax, bluebottles

in the way that your fingers will find the chord
on a piano, knowing the claw-stretch
after years without playing

in the way that the moon will sequester and release
a view of spires and slates
on a bed of staggered indigo

in the way that a man walks out of smoking ruins
clutching his workbag, still wearing
the sameshoes samesuit samecoat as this morning –

in the way that you are falling
through barred cloud, streaked bronze,
dropping like a stone

in the way that we are animals
and our bodies remember things.

Talking to My Mother About Clothes

She knows that she met my father's parents
for the first time in a blue funnel-neck gaberdine coat

can still tell me about the jacket with the fur hood
she treasured when she was eight –

a language that can weather the collapse
of her frontal lobes

of our history,
this pitiless game of hide and seek.

When I fear I'll go the same way
I think of the time we shopped together

in Aberdeen's sprawling TK Maxx
warehouse of frills and flounces,

obscenity of clothes, absurdity of choice:
and we turned at the same time, metres apart,

both holding up
the same plain white linen shirt.

Cluedo

I loved its smallness
(those secret corridors,
that minuscule dagger)
and its bigness (the body
slung across the bannister,
the blood pooling
on the parquet floor)
but most of all
I loved the resolution,
when justice was done
and every piece slotted
neatly back into the box –
as if the world could be
made so tidy; as if
we could pack
any savagery
so carefully away.

Horoscope

This week, expect the unexpected. Perhaps a plague
or a broken nail. You may look closely
at your wristwatch, and inside
          – squint a little, focus! –
there is a world feverishly trying to right itself,
the copper narrowing to a thread,
exposed magnets and whirling subdial.
You might fold yourself up, staring
into the aperture, hunting
the tiny coordinates of your existence:
your stalled figure floating under glass.

Inspector Morse Extra, 1989

On screen for just seven minutes:
I am kissed in an Aston Martin Lagonda
under cherry boughs, wood pigeon calling,

my strapless taffeta gown a poison green.
I'm squired by a ruffle-haired man in a tux,
Tobias? or Lucian? –

perhaps Felix.
My boarding school motto
inscribed on my signet ring:

Fidelis in Parvo.
I have high cheekbones,
hopes of a First. My body

is found two days later:
dragonfly sheen of my sodden dress,
crushed netting between my legs.

Adrift, rolling in the mossy light
under the arches of the Isis,
fingernails full

of the dirt beneath:
                                        o my drowned brain

a colosseum emptying
of all its trapped animals.

Second-Hand Dress

i

I surmise
by the tight bodice
the original owner was narrower than me.
Athletic? Played tennis?

It's an odd colour:
off yellow? Gold-adjacent? Ugly,
but appealing in its vagueness.

Washed twice, it still offers
a hint of musk; violets
sharpening in the heat.

It asks me, constantly,
with every swish of the fabric
who do you think you are?

ii

A confusion of mirrors, prisms.
I watch from a rising escalator:
a shopgirl yawns, then disappears.

Vanishing lines of mannequins,
lipstick bullets in rows:
Strip Me Down, Men Love Mystery.

The dress too tight across my ribs.
Butterscotch, that's the colour.
Mouthful of sweetness, sweetheart.

A Deliverance

I am alone, heartbroken, and on a fast train
sitting in a carriageful of nuns, who are noisier
than you might expect. Italy doesn't know I exist,

but I keep moving from city to city, adoring it all
with the wanton commitment of an ignored lover:
the shuttered *tabaccherie* in the long afternoons;

the jab of morning espresso; starlings circling
another mediaeval church at dusk. My sickness
can't be healed, and prayer has never been my salve

but as I watch the sisters gesticulate,
something starts to mend. Their good faces
rise from their habits like a row of little suns.

For the Mother in the Crowd at Shea Stadium

> 'An announcer stepped to the microphone and said: "Don't worry – the Beatles are here." And from that moment, nobody could hear anything but screams.' – *The Daily News*, August 16, 1965

When the camera veers from the infield diamond,
panning over the audience, you are hard to spot;
outnumbered by your tearstained daughters
who clutch their faces, their hair, grab one another
in a glee that looks closer to pain. It's too hot,
and they are pink-cheeked, toddler-sticky. Severe
in your butterfly-wing glasses, low heels,
and sturdy black handbag, you have the look
of a doctor, one who can dispense
and restore. But they don't turn to you, do they,
these long-limbed, delirious children;
your composure, your dutiful stillness
is what allows them to lurch forward,
screaming, ecstatic, full of fever.

Heliotherapy

Impossible
to grow up here
and not worship the caress,
the muggy dream,
of warmth.

I will show you our altars:

mouthfuls of sand
on wind-lashed beaches

a woman ironing
in her tiny front garden
of parched lawn

men working topless
on scaffolding, in 15 degrees –

tenement windows
all aflare, gleaming

the plain daylight of it

the bowls of our valleys
charged

with sun, damp air
dislodged, all winters

forgiven.

Portraits of Lizzie

i

Her magnificent hair! She catches pneumonia, posing as Ophelia
for John Everett Millais. Shuddering as the bath water cools,
too polite to say the warming lamps have failed.
Fingers shrivelling, teeth starting to chatter.

ii

Rossetti, it must be said, has a receding hairline, but fine whiskers.
He paints Lizzie as Dante's Beatrice: beautiful, unattainable.
Oh, her auburn waves, her trailblazing refusal to wear corsets!
So frail, she's carried into their wedding ceremony.

iii

He is unfaithful. Again. She swallows it all, gossamer poppies
turned liquid. Pregnant, her final overdose.

iv

Rossetti slips a manuscript of his poems into the coils of her hair.
True love. Such devotion! Mourners weep
into crisp laundered handkerchiefs.

v

Seven years pass.

vi

A stray thought as he traces a whorl in his walnut desk.
He calls for tea, knots his brow.
Rossetti wants his poems back.

vii

A ferocity of digging and prising open.

viii

She's the talk of London. Her hair had continued to grow;
coppery sinews fill the box. His book of poems was intact:

ix

aside from a wormhole
(tiny unstoppable tour de force!)
burrowed through every page.

Knapping

knapp (verb – to speak English, as opposed to the Shetland dialect)

When I ask my mother
to translate a word
from Shetlandic

she'll put on
an English accent:
gebe shot? it means

lantern-jawed
and she will stretch
the 'aw' of *jawed*

until it travels
from Mid Yell
eight hundred miles

south, landing
in the grounds
of a Surrey country house,

where *com dee wis*
becomes 'do come in'
and *fulskit* is 'lively'

and *döless*
means 'indolent'
or perhaps, more accurately,
'lacking in ambition or drive'.

The Sonographer Sees the Complication

At first, I thought I was mistaken.
Often there are odd crenulations,
ridges, swirls. But it clarified
as the jellied transducer circled.
It did not look, to me, like a child,
or a kidney stone, or anything human:
it was blinking and starred all around,
complex like latticework.
I knew, then, looking at the patient
she would have to be told:

you have conceived an asterism –
a puzzle of rogue stars,
and you cannot birth them.
They will shrink and condense,
taking you with them,
until you are matter:
lost, minuscule, a twinkle
in the deep curve of a stranger's eye.

Sylvia Plath as Heart Surgeon

Sylvia is the steadiest hand on the team. Early
for every surgery, scrubbing her fingernails,
sporting a surgeon's cap patterned with clowns
(she specialised in paediatric cardiology,
graduating first in her class, after divorcing Ted).

Sylvia sleeps soundly and rises early to bathe
in the ponds at Hampstead Heath.
She likes building fires, the patina of rain on glass,
the way it feels to palpate a tiny heart, the way
it feels to haul small souls back from the light.

Beam

My childhood communion
with flight:
silver and violet diagonals
of my leotard; thud
on scuffed suede; seconds
of weightlessness –

now when I wake,
scrabbling, believing
the daughter we never had
should be in the room
and I can't find her –

deep in my brain's neural pathways
a girl runs light along a beam
launches herself
into chilly air, particles
of chalk spinning
in her wake.

ii

Caddy Lamb

Already, the ewe is disappearing,
ribcage strummed by the wind.
She left behind a fragile-legged lamb,
so weak we have to bottle-feed it.

We approach, clumsy, half-afraid;
my red jersey snags as I climb the fence.
The milk is cold, but she guzzles it down.
We both know it might be kinder

to let her starve –
on that peat-scarred spit of land
she can have only days
before the plunge of a skua or a fox.

On the way home we say nothing
about how long she will last,
or the growing tear
in my sweater. I don't look back

at the scrap of red,
fluttering
above the pitch-dark blanket
of bog and turf.

Revenant Visits Her Old Bedroom

You, stranger, sleep here now.
I present myself at night,
but I have no sinister intention

running a finger along the glass
of milk half-drunk, rim
ghosted with residue.

I may try on your clothes,
buttoning the shirts slowly
as if on vacation.

Here is your desk lamp,
the light lemony, condensed
in an upturned cup of shadow.

I will read your notebooks,
the postcards above your bed.
Here are your hopes

strung up high. Here,
the arrowed sweetness
of your pins and hairclips.

I will leave like anyone else:
stairs, front door, cold grass path
towards the woods.

There I slip from this world
slowly into water:
ankles, knees, waist –

the river thick,
darkly glimmering,
very still.

Sales Pitch of an Honest Estate Agent

The height chart scrawls on the kitchen wall
will acquire a frightening sadness. You will argue

in the bedroom, the kitchen, and in hushed tones
at the bottom of the garden while a barbecue,

complete with popping corks, reaches its climax
closer to the house. In ten years you will ask yourself

if that flooring imported from Rome was worth it –
dovetails of limestone slatted in place

with mathematical precision. The shed
will always smell like resin and old tennis racquets.

Don't imagine for a second
that you'll ever get around to replacing that bath:

an avocado so glossy you could lick it.

Anatomy of a Painting

'Painting is a game of contradictions, of building and destroying.'
– Jenny Saville

She needs full-body lunges to get the curves right. It's faster,
this kind of painting, more viscous: spillages and trickles
as the image is captured and flung against stretched cotton weave.
In the corner, emptied pots of colour: Rose Dorée for lips,
Naples Yellow Light for a swathe of buttery thigh, Cobalt Violet
for veins. Finished, it's vast: rolls of fat, folds and hangings,
waterfalls of human flesh. When she leaves the room,
she abandons teacups, an overspilled ashtray, rags stained
with smears of rust and ochre. But that empty space
recalls something loving – how the tiniest pinprick of cream
can denote light in an eye; the smallest circle of black,
the dip of a belly button.

Opening Scenes of a Never-Made 80s Thriller

The big white house –
a sharp-razored sugarcube
of balcony and glass
the drop
to the spilled turquoise
of a cold pool
filter bubbling
in the hush. Birdsong.

A woman reclines
on a striped lounger:
acid-yellow swimsuit
ten neat toenails painted coral
posed like a mannequin
or a voodoo doll
awaiting pins.

Along the shadow
of a high stucco wall

(alarm disabled, guard dogs silenced)

creeps a man.
No shoes
Hawaiian shirt
gelled hair
reflective aviators.

Before the jump-cut to black
we see her, reflected
in his sunglasses

tiny-boned, oblivious –
one languid leg extended
vivid
as a hummingbird.

Dinner on Ithaca

I should be better at this:
de-shelling a king prawn,
cracking
the lacquered carapace,
running a fingernail
through the digestive tract
trying not to think

downstream, in the treeless dusk
of 1969, my mother finishes a shift
in the crab factory,
a smeared table
of sharp knives.
She's dreaming:

sometimes we'd put our names and addresses
on paper under the wrapping
in the hope that a rich man
would rescue us

Now, they bring raki
flavoured with rosewater,
I lay crumpled notes
next to the bill

dirtsmell of seafood
still on my hands.

Self-Portrait as Submariner

I was not always this way. Once, I gambled
for a bag of tiny fish at a funfair, and swung
the knotted plastic to and fro, all the way home.

I sizzled bream on its back, watched
from a quayside as speckled cod thrashed.
I shimmied a knife under salmon skin,

tucked a linen napkin into my shirt,
cracked open lobster with a little hammer.
Now, I would be more merciful:

I live in the wreckage, though I could slither
through a porthole and leave at my leisure.
The sweeping stair with its rotting carpet,

its vanishing tendrils and swirls. Lacquered panels,
heavy goblets stowed empty as mouths.
At this depth, I am weightless, exploratory:

the grand piano, lid aloft,
canopied with barnacles –
the quiet shoals swimming through.

Kidnap & Escape

When they come for you
you are wearing a satin dress
in cornflower blue,
ochre kidskin slippers
with gilt fastenings.
You do not fight.
You were not raised to fight.

The brougham jolting,
lozenge of light in the cobbled dawn.
Everything a-jangle.
Chitter of diamonds heavy on your earlobes.
Mud-slurry, the horses toiling,
the factory spewing its monstrous cloud.

A big house, emptied out.
You are only a little afraid.

The one left to guard you
has limpid green eyes, defeat
in the set of his shoulders.
After two nights, when you kneel
to open the lock with a hairpin,
you see the high polish
of his black boots. He is snoring,
or pretending to.

You burst into a fine garden
hemmed by walls, scrabble for a door
under a mantle of ivy and moss.
Finally, battered oak and a rusted ring.
The handle slowly turning. Beyond,
the river fattening in its girdle,
and the frosted road
where you hail a horse and rider,
point north. Just a small run
in your silk stockings.

Blackbird

What are you, to yourself? A missile
of muscle, feather and bone, twitch
in scuffed leaves, a fine-ringed eye?

Dim warble of dawn, sharp cossetting
of a nest, a ruffle among siblings.
Loop-the-loop through ebullient cloud,

swallow of long worms in soft dirt.
Speckled shells beginning to crack,
calculated landings. Folded wings in rain.

Ghazal for a Small Town

Wild garlic, damp coolness
of the overgrown woods, deep tangle

of the road south. Moon hung in the mist.
My mother unplaiting my sister's hair tangle.

Shafts of light bisecting the library stacks.
We test ourselves: vodka, cigarettes, untangling

our limbs from childhood bonds. Dented bracelet
of the bay encircling the sea; wild tangle

of seaweed, bladderwrack. Beached jellyfish.
It will take me years to untangle this:

a muddied helix of love and stillness,
those hours of boredom tangled with joy.

Animal Magnetism

> 'The somnambulists were completely insensible ... we might pinch their skin, prick them with pins under the nails etc, without their even perceiving it.'
>
> – *Royal Academy of Medicine Commission on Mesmerism*, Paris, 1825

Lines of fragile, excited women,
armpits darkening with sweat.
The private back room
rendered uncertain
by dripping candlelight;
warmth tempered
by an erratic draft.
Outside, rain like lambswool
deadening the sound,
the chittering queues.

Your trance is pellucid.
You see everything:
buckets of fishguts
in your mother's kitchen;
the corona of foxgloves outside your church;
dots of blood on your crêpe de Chine
from a failed mending; how you have flailed.
How you have slipped
through the years, a good girl,
temperate, accommodating –

his hand is pressed upon your crown.
You can do nothing about it now.

Domestic

Swift tie and untie of apron. Years
of slipping away as a well-scrubbed hand
touches your hip. Pewter-grey dawns
on your knees with the hearth billowing
ash and soot. Cold. Thin blankets,
mice scrabbling, the attic window
veiled with ice. Not seeing or hearing:
arguments, thrown champagne glasses,
bloodied sheets. Thinning memories
of home, of the huddle of cottages
fifty miles away, distant as the moon.
Fortnightly hair-washing, coil of grease
pinned at the nape of your neck. Acres
of parquet buffed to a painful sheen.
Letters home. *Dear Mother and Father,*
how are you? I am very well. Yesterday,
we had junket with blackberries.

Japanese Wind Telephone

for Peter

When you asked me for a love poem
I told you about a glass booth

containing one object,
a disconnected rotary phone:

black, shiny as whale belly,
from which the grieving

can dial the numbers
of their lost ones, speak

to the listening dead.
I promised

that after you were gone,
I would keep telling you things:

how our children are growing;
how the blown apple blossom

fills the gutter
outside our house;

how our neighbours
still make love so loudly

and when they wake me
I find I have reached again

for your hand.

Afternoon Tea in a Time of Horror and Chaos

Lightning claws open a sky
milky
like an offered bowl

diminishing the garden's peacock
to a flash of tail-feather
framed by stained-glass doors.

Ignore each strike embellishing
and dimming the room,
making the china stutter.

Cut into sponge
sodden with syrup,
tease apart sticky dates.

Sip, swallow,
as hammering rain
darkens the flagstones.

When the maid offers
to lower the blinds, say
no, there is no need. Say

plump the cushions
at my back, please. Call
for a fresh jug of cream.

Blót

Blót (Old Norse): a sacrifice in exchange for gods' goodwill,
in battle, weather or fertility, for example

You navigate a foreign language:
dummy transfer, antral follicle count,
ovarian hyperstimulation syndrome.

In the pethidine-dark struggle and relapse
you dream illuminated manuscripts,
tranquil stacks: the world of the brain

a making
a making you could undertake
not this brutal physicality.

They say *the egg retrieval went well.*
The pain is so bad you throw up.
Scent of disinfectant, pinkish:

wake in a sea of your own blood.
You will rise up
from the ruins of your body

from the altar piled with needles,
thumbed-out pill packets,
from a decade of longing

precise as unslaked thirst.

iii

Life Model

after Lisel Muller

If I moved an inch,
I would crack like a glaze.

My body plucked of clothes, rendered
in blotchy shades of chickpea and ballet slipper.

Hours arrayed in a sliver of breeze, pinpricks
of flesh rising on my thighs.

Stray hair over my eye nagging
like a half-remembered tune. Stilled

by the fourth-floor light
from the high art-room windows, I'd listen

to the city's plainsong,
its honeycomb clamour.

No matter how long I'd lie there,
some parts they could never get right:

sunspot on my cheek, mole at my elbow,
the scar meandering over my heart.

This Is a True Story

I would not marry into that house.
I couldn't condemn
my unconceived children
to their strange bloodline:
oddly shaped ears, a mad uncle,
small boys packed off to Eton,
and an imperious matriarch
reigning over the tea-table.
God, the mother loved to bake.
I was suspicious of her flirtation
with domesticity, seeing as
they had *staff*, but she was a pro
with the first incision,
opening up Victoria sponge
like a neurosurgeon,
and she'd wave that knife in the air,
if she disliked the conversation.
I marvelled at their gift
for turning near-miss into legend:
He almost rowed for Oxford, you know!
Giles practically climbed Everest in '92!
Years later, I found a photo of us,
grinning for the camera
at a gleaming tea-table.
I'd told the story to so many –
this incredibly rich family! –
that I could barely recall
how much of it was theirs,

and how much mine. I confess,
the Mater held no scalpel
in the shot; the light was kind,
the cakes appeared delicious,
and all their ears looked fine.

Bellville, TX

The town came out for it: corn on the cob,
rippling flags, sweat on cooling cans.

Streets narrowing with flesh.
Candy stacked like apples, the stricken line

of the highway east. Sun stitching the wound
of deep-ploughed fields.

Iced tea in a plastic glass:
the morning's easy weight.

That unlit corner – a hand in the leaves
in the garden of a dead man.

Those in line for the Ferris wheel
were restless and happy.

I too was waiting, under green vines,
for my life to detonate in front of me –

overhearing the psychic in her stifling tent,
The Hierophant, The Hermit, The High Priestess.

Swimming

I never loved anything as I love that first immersion in salt,
the sand shelving, dipping through ribbons of tepid and cool.
Strange that I, so fearful, would want the mystery of it,
haul of tide, tangle of bladder-wrack at my feet,
trailing fronds. The pink bathers on the shoreline
shrink and shrink again, aligning their towels,
unpacking picnic boxes of smaller boxes: juice, crackers, raisins.
The blue deepening, pulling, as I spot my family waving
from a sickle of sand, contained in a cowl of blinding light.

The Dead Go to the Theatre

Curtain up! The dead
have corralled their bones
for the spectacle.

Here's a world so lush,
vividly coloured in plum,
carmine and gold –

flecks of glitterball light
hit a collarbone here,
an ulna there.

Interval. They minnow
toward the orchestra pit,
reach into a tuba's dark mouth

run a tongue along
a rosined viola string.
Every pot of ice cream

will have a tiny scoop
taken from it. Backstage
they stir chaos:

clouds of face powder,
greasepaint on the wigs.
At the final curtain, the dead

want only what we want:
the best of them
still sit among us, arrayed

in their splendidly polished shoes.

Icarus as a Girl

Vivid, the lit flicker
of each gauzy wing:
every hair
on the back of my neck
catches alight,
my locks kindle
from damp flax
to flaming torch

I drop

bare arms flapping,
useless.

The story
has been mistold.
I'm girl, not boy,
got further than you think
(that giddy soar, that scrape
of the fireball's cusp)

invincible. Or not;
this flailing mess
of feather and wax.
Who's to say
what I cry out
as I plummet?

Who's to say
how it sounds,
the glaze
and crackle
of my skin?

Cassiopeia

i.

Pregnancy gave me no stretch marks
only a constellation
of new freckles across my ribcage

where inside, another ribcage formed
tiny harp
matchstick cathedral

all those nights, dreaming
his string-of-pearls spine
the wild complexity of artery and vein

the deep pit of fear at my throat.
I clawed my way through
with a prize held high

starlit band, fine netting,
open clusters
luminous in the gloaming.

Even as ribbons of returning sun
lay their fingers across my chest
I stream into that rayless sky

the darkness I wanted so badly:
Sagittarius releasing arrow after arrow
Cassiopeia, arrogant and lush –

ii.

Is it vanity to love my body more now?
Its widened hips, a new pink line,
sibling to the heart-scar

where they cranked open my chest
fixed me four decades ago
by splicing my pomegranate heart?

(Once a new lover took off my clothes and gasped,
horrified: *what happened to you?*
Nothing, I wanted to say. *Everything.*)

On Suburbia

What I'm trying to say is the sputter
of lights on the dual carriageway
viewed from the empty playing fields
in the dark; the rows of bungalows
we longed to escape from then
worked so hard to return to;
our children drowsing
under canopies of plastic stars;
every kitchen appliance at rest,
obedient, the thrum of a normality
so rickety it could crack any second;
the tiptoed pause at the door
listening to them breathe;
how this is love,
or what I know of it, right now.

Son, it's 7pm in April

and whatever is next
you should know
the slowness and care
of your father as he tends to you
his broad back and shoulders
        generations of farmhands
        tilling fields in the dirt, in all weathers,
        men made for life's heavy lifting
those wide fingers
labouring zips and buttons,
patient hours with your vellum cheek
lolling on his shoulder,
as we black out the rising spring,
the blackbird's skittish chorus.

Sweetheart

I want to make you good things.
To simmer and fold
until cream and sugar clot
into caramel; to roll and unmould
dainty madeleines or macarons.
It's no use. I'm better at pickles,
ribbons of courgette cut and plunged
into vinegar. Show me love,
and I'll show you hands smeared
with vermillion chilli, crushed garlic,
splinters of ginger
under every fingernail.

The Charity Shops of Aberdeen

October. The boredom of loitering
while my mum went through the rails
with high-speed concentration:

the focus of those who love clothes
and know overdrafts. She had an eye
for Aztec prints, bracelet-length sleeves,

anything *real* – silk, leather, wool.
I learned from those coppery afternoons
scented by instant coffee and damp coats:

now, the best thing in my wardrobe
has a 60s Neiman Marcus label,
a batwing top, all hand-stitched sequins,

possibly worn by a long-dead
martini-swilling divorcée. A useful piece
that announces itself

before you open your mouth.
Isn't this the truth of us;
the things we lust after?

The dream of transformation
in every new waist or neckline,
that gorgeous, refracted autumn light.

The Calligrapher

When you began to work in lampblack, vitriol, narcissus liquor,
you thought you might escape the material world;
thought those covers of blind-tooled goatskin, the half-life
of liquid drying into immortality, might offer redemption –

but all you found were callouses, fading sight,
a tiny fleet of ghost ships sent into the mist.

Man with Hidden Face

In the dreams you are never one thing.
Sometimes you are a sculptor, chiselling
marble into submission: or a surgeon,
with your scalpel and covered mouth;
in another dream you ride for miles over desert
with the sun at your back, a Stetson low over your eyes;
or you captain a ship, roll it alongside icebergs
so close your passengers can reach out a fingernail
and scratch the ice. In none of the dreams
do you have a name, but in one of them
you leave a note in the grass, scored
deep into the soil with a sharpened stick,
and in that note, you explain everything –
name, blood type, catalogue of sins,
penances, sports affiliations,
what frightens you at night.

Vesta Surveys Pompeii

I'm sorry. To this day
I don't know why I did it.
You are still clutching dice
from the morning's game,
curled under a table
which holds a glazed bowl
of eggs, perfectly preserved.

The mosaic tiles at the door
read *cave canem*. Your dog
with its hot breath,
its readied claws,
suffocated too.

Nights, I dream
of inhaling the wreckage,
gathering the spilled lava
and torrent of stone
into my own body

until mouths and ears
unclog, people stand,
dust themselves off,
and speck by speck
all my damage is undone.

The Patron Saint of Lost Things

As I sit with my love in the pew, his knowledge makes him foreign:
when to stand, when to bow your head and murmur *Amen*.

I don't recognise his face as he shakes hands at the head of the line,
the hush of mourners saying *sorry for your trouble, sorry for your loss,*

so sorry, god bless. As a child, he was always the one to find things:
lost keys, the dog's lead, loose change for mass. I think of him

running child-speed through the rooms that now sit dark,
hunting at the gravel-lined edge of the garden next to her lavender,

under her neatly made bed, or in her press full of laundered sheets.

Miniature

I've been working so late
on this matchstick version
of our neighbourhood:

its tenement rows, the bungalows
around the park. I melt sweets
to make the church's stained glass;

its amber so translucent,
like skin held too close
to light. I soften wax

over flame to seal the corners,
cover it with my arms
when traffic shudders outside.

The cobbled streets are made
with pomegranate seeds
sucked free from their casing,

and every shop in the arcade
contains stick people, fashioned
with pins and neat twists

of my own hair. Each time
I think it's complete, another
street occurs to me, another

remembered office block
or swimming pool. So many years
have passed since I began;

it is damaging my eyes, hunching
my spine. When I set it alight,
I will pay attention as it kindles

to a blaze of scarlet and black,
so I can write it, remake it,
as the buildings flatten to ash.

The Pantone Colour of the Year is Green 2252c

I want to live
with green things
all around me
the chartreuse
of early crocus
the mantis
of a football pitch
the cyan
of sea-glass
gathered from the ebb
the pistachio
of softly folded gelato
the myrtle
of blown branches
starting to bud
in all this green
I will sleep
waking
to a hysteria
of birdsong

56.9° North

On the coiling road in
you pull over, stop the car,
and just look at it – contained,
gleaming in the evening sun.
The war memorial is cloaked
in shadow, flanked by fields
in saffron and seaweed-green,
those huddled woods you know
are thick with wild garlic.

The harbour's cupped hands.

You wait, as if by watching
you could spool the film backwards,
shrink yourself into the life
you once inhabited. This
is not your home any more. But

if someone asked you right now
what is it that you love?
you'd say this town, as it was
and as it is now, aflame in the dusk:
the crumbling path to the castle,
the old pool empty, padlocked,
waiting for the salt
of another summer.

The End

This is how I imagine it. Twilight.
Trees stripped of their leaves,
clouds unbraiding themselves
dissolving into billows of silk,
shreds of desiccated coconut.
The low bushes swagged with late berries.

Two children run past
with toy walkie-talkies.
You are happy. You greet
strangers with ruddy cheeks
collecting conkers. The path
beneath your feet is crunchy,
the colour of old pennies.

You reach a library,
set neatly on an oblong
of frosted lawn. Inside,
silence, the musk of old books,
a cantilevered staircase
and a ceiling ribbed
in palest blue.

Pienza

When we stopped for shade in a courtyard –
cold mosaic tiles, baskets of jasmine –
we opened water bottles and stale *pasticcini*
and talked about the hike up and how small
the town was and how happy we were
to be asked for directions on the road
though we could only say *non siamo di qui*
and shrug. The air was thick with birdsong,
incense and (somewhere) weed and then
we heard the singing, a choir, no instruments,
an old, crumpled priest conducting younger priests
the light seemed whiter and more radiant
falling on the graffiti and chipped ochre and blue;
we froze with our lukewarm water and pastries
afraid to move in case we disturbed them –
it was heaven. I am telling you now
it was heaven and we had no idea.

Mijas Pueblo

Let the lemons ripen on their trees; let those that drop
fleck with rot and house insects. Shutter the windows,
double lock the door. The sun will still crawl
up over the horizon; patient blinkered donkeys
will clip through cobbled streets, and each morning
when the tide tows its mist back towards the deep,
a black-clad woman will sweep up debris in the square:
cherry blossom, ice-cream wrappers, or discarded tickets
from the bull-ring, where cheap seats are marked
sol and expensive ones *sombra*. There will be celebrations,
the little church encircled by bridal flowers, wreaths.
The village will go on without you, revolving
in its unremarkable remarkable way, as rain falls,
cooler dusks come, and the tethered animals
turn and sigh in their stalls.

Acknowledgements

Big thanks to the editors of the magazines, journals and anthologies who published some of the poems in this collection: *Ambit*, *Best Scottish Poems*, *Butcher's Dog*, *The Honest Ulsterman*, *The Interpreter's House*, *The Keats-Shelley Review*, *Magma*, *Mslexia*, *The New Shetlander*, *Nutmeg*, *The Oxford Magazine*, *The Passionfruit Review* and *The Scotsman*.

Some of these poems were written in New York at Poets House (thanks to the Scottish Graduate School for Arts and Humanities) and in Krakow, Poland (thanks to Justyna Joachim and the UNESCO Cities of Literature programme).

Love and thanks to my publisher, Duncan Lockerbie, my agent Caro Clarke, and to the friends and mentors who worked on many of these poems with me: Tim Craven, Miriam Gamble, Rebecca Goss, Russell Jones, Dorothy Lawrenson, Marianne Macrae, Jane McKie, Lauren Pope, Helen Tookey.

And to my family – thank you. I love you beyond words.